In the Months of My Son's Recovery

Southern Messenger Poets

DAVE SMITH, SERIES EDITOR

In the months of my son's recovery

POEMS

Kate Daniels

LOUISIANA STATE UNIVERSITY PRESS
BATON ROUGE

Published by Louisiana State University Press
Copyright © 2019 by Kate Daniels
All rights reserved
Manufactured in the United States of America
LSU Press Paperback Original

Designer: Michelle A. Neustrom
Typeface: Whitman
Printer and binder: LSI

Library of Congress Cataloging-in-Publication Data

Names: Daniels, Kate, 1953– author.
Title: In the months of my son's recovery : poems / Kate Daniels.
Description: Baton Rouge : Louisiana State University Press, [2019] | Series:
    Southern messenger poets
Identifiers: LCCN 2018036785 | ISBN 978-0-8071-7035-9 (pbk. : alk. paper) |
    ISBN 978-0-8071-7149-3 (pdf) | ISBN 978-0-8071-7150-9 (epub)
Classification: LCC PS3554.A5636 A6 2019 | DDC 811/.54—dc23
LC record available at https://lccn.loc.gov/2018036785

for

Mona Frederick & Arleen Tuchman

They carried me through . . .

contents

i. Her

ii. The Addict's Mother

iii. Him

iv. Us

A NOTE TO READERS

These poems are narrated by a character similar, but not identical, to myself, and represent other characters and situations that may be archetypal, emanating from many aspects of and perspectives on the current opioid epidemic.

i. Her

(Where can you find a place
to keep her, with all the huge strange thoughts inside you
going and coming and often staying all night.)

—RAINER MARIA RILKE

Her Barbaric Yawp

I sound my barbaric yawp over the roofs of the world.

—W. WHITMAN

Past time to praise that beautiful freak,
the aging Female Body. It was easy to praise her
back in the day, watching her celebrate and sing
herself on TV, in movies, on billboards and glossy
printed ads, in the narcissistic privacies
of our ceiling-mirrored beds and baths
where we met her in our own fresh images. Young,
clad all over in tight, unwrinkled skin, not yet
stretched out or sagging, she was a pleasure
to ogle . . . So we gawked and gaped
as she flung her diaphragm, unwashed,
in the corner of a bedroom at party's end,
then mated, again, in the dirt, peeling the used
condom from the sole of her boot,
and walked out to breakfast, bra-less in a thin
tee shirt and someone's boxer shorts tightened up
at the waist with a safety pin.
                                        What a beauty
she was back then, what a marvel—butchered
haircuts grew out quickly, and the godawful blood-
streaked whites of eyes and puffy cheeks
of all-night benders gave way uncomplainingly
to a good night's sleep and extra hydration.
Just that, and the young beast was ready to roar again . . .

Well, *that's* all decades in the past. Now,
there's this flowing away, this gigantic
ongoing flush she finds herself fighting.
The juice that made it all go, the oil,

the universal lubricant that used
to grease the gears of all
that made her *her* is runneling down
the body's hidden culverts.
And eating more salads, giving up
hard cheese, or taking on red wine,
even adding extra sessions of Pilates
won't do a goddamn thing to change it.

*

Who would blame her for being angry
and noncompliant? For missing
the not-quite-greasy wetness of excitation
that *doesn't get around all that much anymore* . . .
Trying to re-arouse it, she thinks of the pugnacious
bitchiness of Etta James singing the old jazz song,
affirming how *awfully different life is* without
the old companions of her youth—the low growling
deep in the gut when potential mates sauntered
into view, and the way that nothing more than that
image unleashed the hydraulic blood rush
that scurried to the center of the marshy pelt
where she used to keep her privacy.

*

Everywhere she lugs it,
these days, the old beast feels strange
and unwelcome, uninfused by fresh blood
as inert and useless as a stretched-out elastic strip
undone from the waistline by too many washings . . .

Those cloying fresh fish and damp mold
smells she used to try to soak and scrape
off herself are history now. What she wouldn't give
to have them back . . . And that patch
of skin on the side of her neck where her first date
placed his fingers midway through the movie
whispering in wonder *your skin's so soft* ?
that's the slackened flap she gathers up
and pulls back, in front of the bathroom
mirror, rehearsing a lift.

*

The word BITCH leaps out at her now
from many contexts. And every single
time she hears or reads it, she gets
a little shock. Her old dog back home
on the living room sofa, spayed and tranquilized
by domesticity, trying to keep warm in the winter sun—
dear god, don't even go there . . .

*

All the new thinking's about loss,
so opined a famous male poet in 1981—
something at the time she didn't comprehend.
Now it comes back full force, motoring
through the brand new millennium,
soundtracked by the male gender's
elegiac yawping about all they've lost:
submissive spouses and cowed kids;
the ability to control the flow of urine,
to achieve and sustain a workable
erection; the freedom to compete for jobs
unhindered by dark-skinned applicants uplifted
a bit by affirmative action . . .

She, too, is thinking about loss. Nothing new
there, however: loss of weight, loss of looks, long
perished virginity. Loss of reputation/job opportunity/
promotion/raise. Loss of one or both breasts,
then the entire reproductive system removed
in a prophylactic surgery that may not succeed.
Loss of hair following chemotherapy. Then
loss of libido, and loss of long-term partner,
repulsed by the scar site's topography.

*

All those packs of older women
at the movies together, in restaurants,
padding about in their Reeboks
and fanny packs on single sex
organized tours of the offbeat capitals
of eastern Europe. She hates the tacky
attraction of their freedom even as
she craves it. No more makeup
or sucking in her gut. No more worrying
about what her husband used to caution her
about: "the old male ego" when she aced him
consistently on the tennis court.

*

Ok: she admits she wants the juice back,
but does that make her a failed
feminist? To crave the juice again,
but without the bother? How bad
was the bother anyway?

Now that it's over, marriage keeps
drifting back in concise forms and piercing
images she can't dismiss: hefty handfuls
of warm man-parts under the covers
of their bed, and that cheesy smell
in his trousers that never laundered out.
Him hauling garbage out in rain and snow,
handling the metal cans with bare hands
in slick sleet. The dip stick whose greasy
level he always understood. And beneath the lamp
in the dining room, reading glasses tilted
on his nose, paying bills the first of each month.
He was the necessary mind of math,
and she was something less precise,
but richer and more complex. The full range,
perhaps, of the arts and humanities . . .

*

At the pool, years ago . . .

A flash of pure hatred had inflated her
when the flat-bellied one in the two-piece
swimsuit murmured to her friend, *I'm glad I'm
past that,* nudging her head at her swollen stomach.

And she had glared, and positioned the tremendous
ass of the eighth month of her second pregnancy
to block the view, and waddled off slowly, plowing
warlike through the world with her magical body.

*

Once, she had contained
multitudes of milk and meat
that her body turned to bones and blood:
living orbs she carted heavily about
until she couldn't bear it anymore,
and they slithered out, covered in slime
and already mewling, thrilling her with ancient
emotions that filtered through as if brand new.

Now the orbs reside in southern California,
struggling with bad air and property tax.
Ungrammatically, they whine in texts and emails
until she tunes them out, and falls back
from the glowing screens, to gorge
on inward images of their infancies
when she sucked and licked them
at her leisure, undressed them solely
to admire her corporeal handiwork, then
clamped them to her tits to shut them up,
and pumped out effortlessly the milky
sustenance of human life . . .

*

The fucking head won't fit!
Her profane utterance
at the moment of crowning
as her son's head descended,
striving to spill from the hole ripped
open between her legs . . .

*

The café was crowded,
and the young couple
had nowhere to sit.
Strategizing, they hovered,
hands full of food.

Right above our heads, the male
muttered, *Wish one of these
hags would pick up her broom
and fly away.* And the young
female tittered . . .

It's because we're old,
Mona had said compassionately,
gesturing at her own face
as if to soften the blow to mine.
They don't even see us anymore . . .

*

Trapped in the climacteric, bad physics
reigns. Suddenly, seasons are flowing in reverse
—spring is returning to winter—and she's
unraveling backwards across time
to ankle socks and unshaved legs,
to un-bloodstained panties, and the box
of napkins not yet needed, secretly stored
on the closet floor. Stepping tentatively again
into the museum gallery of her own young body—
how reverently she stood before the mystery
back then, meditating on the double shrine
of eggs-in-waiting, the swaying clusters that swung
like grapes about to be cut from the vine.

*

She's always appreciated the double X,
and never was aware of wanting anything other
than her own moist nest of fur and smell.
Certainly not an obtruding, mauled-up club
of alternating hard/soft flesh dangling between
her legs, or the social privileges it's alleged to confer.

        Her analyst (of course)
thought otherwise. It escapes her now
why she spent those three long years, hoarding
her secret on his scratchy couch: how much she loved
her fleshy crevices, and the personal thrill
the first time her finger slipped inside
and how claimed she was then, how permanently
imprinted by the moist and clinging secrets
of female subjectivity . . .

*

Her old relationship with the toilet bowl
has finally ended. No more kaleidoscopic clots
of unconceived children sliding out
month after month. No more
fleshy smells of fresh come wafting up
from dropped panties. No more
thighs greasily sliding on the toilet seat
eased by spermicide mixed with semen.

Time to accept she'll never drop
those clots of blood again deep
into the swirling waters, and stare down,
mesmerized by the images of fleeing
half-lives that might have come
to resemble her own . . .

Just piss now, ordinary
as rain. Humble and unpretentious
as sweat.
　　　　　No, wait.
　　　　　　　Sometimes
there's still a little vinegary thrill
at the end, a final, rage-filled spurt
that splits apart the storage compartments
of the aging beast, and riles up
the old memories archived
deep inside the nearly all used-up,
but *still* commodious
female body . . .

Anorexia Nervosa

i

Now that it's fall, they've hauled
their difficult beauty—all sharp edges
and shiny joints—back onto campus.

Before our eyes, they're changing
into something no one understands
but them and the other members

of their strange clan. Gleeful hoarders,
clandestine calculators, secretly they subtract
themselves, calorie by calorie, crumb

by crumb, gram of fat by gram
of fat—disappearing in plain sight, devouring
themselves by devouring nothing . . .

Poured perfectly into brief skirts
and tight capris, their taut flanks
and ridged bellies ripple beneath

the wandering hands of fleshy boys
in caps worn backwards. On party
nights, barely anything's required

to get them drunk. And so they dance,
flying high above the earthbound burden
of the tiny bodies they're dying to erase.

In the cafeterias, they perch among us,
primeval, girl-size birds of prey, nibbling
skittishly on leftover bits that anyone

else would throw away. Visualize
a vulture and its ducked, pink head, targeted
on lunch, and you'll see the similarity

—bony shoulders hunched above almost
empty trays, hooded eyes, claw-like
fingers pecking at undressed bowls

of salad greens. *They must be starving.*
That's the trite thought that fills our heads
as we stuff ourselves, looking away to avoid

the violence their images discharge—the sharp
angles and dessicated volumes of shed flesh,
the vacant bellies and caved-in cheeks

they slash us with . . .

ii

Some girls tat themselves up to mark
their difference—and walk about *that* way,
flaunting the world's girl-shaming, persecutory gaze,

egging it on, using their bodies to invite altercations
they're confident they'll win. The starving girls
size it up differently, their fragilities lacking

the right words to say it. What use are words
when so many can't read, others won't,
and almost no one cares anymore

for carefully crafted utterance . . . Images
still slay however, driving themselves deep
in the center where language peters out

and words merge new territories, spreading
into flat puddles, all color and shape. What can't
be given voice still announces itself in other mediums:

Painted or draped on the human body.
Or carved into a girl's sweet flesh with a straight
edge blade she's hidden in the bathroom

and takes to herself, after vomiting
her dinner.

iii

Some madness—is divinest sense.
The Divine Miss D. opined this, waxing psychoanalytic
decades before Freud's famous theory.

It fills my head now—the sense in madness,
the madness in sense—as my student sits
beside me, protesting her right to have an opinion.

This is probably wrong, she says. *Probably
stupid,* twisting her hair, and shrinking back
in the chair I have positioned so close

She won't be able to escape when I need
to remind her she's more than her body.

iv

Mommy, what is my mind?
My daughter asked me
When she was three.

Strapped in her car seat.
Tapping her temple
As I sometimes do

When I'm writing
A poem, or trying
To think.

A kind of machine,
Was what I said.
You can use it

To build things.
Like ladders,
Or cars.

v

Journal excerpts, over the years . . .

Why has miniaturization mostly been a woman's art?

　　*

What exactly is the male attraction to the 20-inch waist?

*

Keeping things small, and manageable: that's
one way *I've* kept breakdown at bay.

*

Sometimes life is too large to even imagine
what might be required to extract oneself
from the master plot.

*

Found Sonnet from November 9, 1999

Today, _____ , my favorite student in poetry class,
Fainted in my office. One second, she was upright,
Discoursing on the unexpected pleasures
Of Frost's blank verse. The next, her eyelids
Retracted in her head. Hands twitching,
She fell from her chair, and slid to the floor
And I thought she was dead. Before I reached her,
She was coming back, apologizing. (They always *do*
Apologize.) "I'm sorry, Professor," she kept on saying.
"I haven't eaten a thing today. My parents are paying me
A lot of money to lose some weight before the break.
We're going on a cruise with my stepfather's family."

Then she made it worse: "And they're all very thin."
"I'm sorry, Professor," she apologized again.

*

In the course called "Existentialism," the exam was only two questions:

1. Define *dread*.
2. Describe *horror*.

*

For god's sake, stop rubbernecking, and read the text!

Homage to Frank O'Hara:
Fire Island Tea Dance, Summer '78

> To be idiomatic in a vacuum,
>
> it is a shining thing!
>
> —FRANK O'HARA

i

This was back when sex was still mainly personal,
something reliable enough to transform random
moments, exciting as an uncapped glass of gasoline
in one hand and a lit match flickering in the other,
bumbling drunk down a rocky path in the dark . . .
                                    It was the end time
of old time, old school, uncomplicated sex before
sex became political, before it was a "choice,"
before it was renamed "safe" and "unsafe,"
before it had starved itself down to late night
exercise for staving off boredom, before it
wrapped itself up as a goodbye gift to a long-
term partner, before it was as casual as saying
ciao, or who the hell *are* you, anyway,
or a pick-me-up for one's own pitiful self,
struggling through a tough patch at the office,
or moving, all but narcoleptic, through the endless
dooms of an aged parent's diminishing . . .

All those decades ago, you would have said,
it was spiritual. *Sex is spiritual.* (*Yes, that was you
back then.*) And thought of looking straight into a pair
of eyes at the all-important moment of climax
as the thrilling pinnacle of making love. Really, though,
all you could have meant, unleavened as you were,
was something mathematical, an uninformed

rave-up of randomness, two bodies coincidentally
colliding instead of sliding right past each other
in the vast nothingness you learned in "Existentialism
101" to call the *Zero at the Center of It All.*

Pretentious girl . . . How stubbornly you clung
to your English major's *cri de coeur:* that meaning
inhered in the tight forms straining in the heat of every
coupling was something you insisted on back then,
buttressing your argument with bawdy passages
from Whitman, and lines of Rilke. *Every angel
is terrifying.* So when your lover pushed you
roughly down on the floor of his parents' den,
and thrust himself inside you, uninvited, and covered
your cries with his hand, obliterating your plea
in the soft crush of a sofa cushion, afterwards you
cleaned up the blood, and rifled through your repertoire
of limited reactions and chose something "poetic."

The new soreness (*you told yourself*) was a wonder . . .

ii

Crossing over on the ferry to Fire Island Pines, the engines
thrum so hard up your thighs the raw tufts of your week-old
bikini wax tremble in their nest of tender skin, and you can feel
the new wound throbbing. It is calming somehow to pull out
the already dog-eared, thumbed-up copy of Frank O'Hara's
Selected Poems, still almost new, and to run your fingers
along the pages' greasy selvage. Now *there* was a person
who understood sex, and had practiced his knowledge
on the island puttering into view. A long fringe of frilly
pines appears, wind-ruffled, like cut-off bangs, smearing

the clear space of a woman's forehead. You press yourself
back in the last seat on the top deck, shielding your eyes
with your hand because it's too bright, really, too bright
to see and because maybe, after all, you don't want to see—

The engine roars in reverse, then the ferry backs up weakly
paralleling the dock. You glimpse yourself: sole woman
in a clan of men. Not quailing, but shy, like a girl
who hides herself behind her thumb or hair.
Or a tensed-up coed, over conscious of her monthly
smell. Thus marked, you disembark in the narrow
weirdness of all one gender, and walk, zipped inside
that conformity, side by side but out of sync with your brothers,
tapping along the wooden planks to find your path.

iii

The plan was to lie naked on the beach—for the first
Time ever—researching the Male Gaze, establishing

The conditions necessary for stepping out
Of the loathsome self-awareness of the female

Gender. You hypothesized it might be as
Liberating as undoing a long-stuck zipper, freed

By lubricant, embracing the exuberant
Gushing as it rushes down, spilling open to

Occupy a space where there are no thieves . . .

                    Is that even
                    possible?

iv

Out there, on the ocean's shore, the hour of exposure
                              slouched round.

You had polished your jewels, and carefully curated
the exhibition. So you stepped down onto the beach,
and drew out the terry cloth towel, and flapped it
sharply in the air and spread it flat on hot sand.
As tenderly as if you were your own first lover,
you removed your clothes and lay down flat
to display yourself beneath the sun, plied open,
gritty bits of hot sand drifting deep inside
your magical crevices and your salty clefts,
                              waiting . . .

And nothing happened but the hot burning of sun
on exposed skin that had never felt a direct ray,
or been cooled by the salt spray of ocean waves
that infiltrated the hot air, relieving it slightly.

                      All around you, naked men
moved, rubbing lotions into each other, cupping
their hands to rearrange sweaty piles of male loins
uncomfortably swollen in the heat. How irrelevant
your own loins felt. How impersonal to be extracted,
excised from the mainstream text, then put back down,
sidelined in the margins of an encyclopedic volume
you'd never even read . . .

As if it were an outdoor laboratory dedicated
to the study of gender identity, or an open air
museum's solo show on the female self as some

old man's Muse: the beach obliterated received ideas.
The sun was impassive and objective. Purely scientific,
it sharpened its focus until it brought you into view
as the object of desire for no one but your Self—a thought
so radical you almost choked. Then old paradigms
fell apart, and new images churned to the surface:
Mind: a genderless cloud. *Body:* a rickety pile
of anthropomorphic sticks that's carried you about
all these years not caring if it wears a penis or vagina.

Enclosed in the bell jar of new blank space, go ahead
and claim for yourself a sand angel's queerness,
naked on the hot beach, winging both arms
to carve new boundaries—

v

The afternoon tea dance in the open air pavilion
is semi-raging when you enter—still solitary, still
female. Casual gazes greet you, then move on
quickly, neither dismissive nor predatory—nothing
more than one person taking casual note of another.

vi

Postscript: Dear Frank,
Thanks to you, *I am breathing the pure
Sphere* of freedom from The Gaze,
Here in the place where you perished
Authentic and queer to the very end.

ii. The Addict's Mother

With what, exactly, would you expect to frighten me?

—DENIS JOHNSON

In the Midst of the Heroin Epidemic

When I heard the news that Cynthia's daughter
had died, all alone, slumped over on the ground
beside a dumpster behind the convenience store
where she'd made her final buy, I logged off, and
walked outside to look at the water before I could think
too much. It's become a habit now—losing myself
in the soothing image of moving water before the headlines
and the stats start blaring out the way they do—performing
themselves inside my mind that has always imagined
too vividly too much . . . *You think too much,* my parents
always said. But thinking about this, or not thinking
won't reverse the events that have captured Cynthia
or bring back the daughter who's been carried away
in an opening chapter of a terrible plot. Addicts destroy
themselves—that's just where we start. And why
they might have wanted to, or if it was an accident
is beside the point . . . The aftermath is what's at stake.
The human flotsam captured in addiction's filthy wake.
Ordinary citizens like Cynthia with her stone face
and her dead blue eyes. Single mother of one child,
deceased. She works at the bakery down the block
from me. I pay her for a cappuccino and a buttered roll
every morning on my way to work. Afterwards,
I linger on the wooden pier, and drown my eyes
in the river's watery embrace, and lick butter
from my fingers, and fill my head with the strong smell
of hot coffee Cynthia poured for me. Small actions
that distract. They minimize, but can't efface,
any of the suffering.

The Addict's Mother: Birth Story

She wasn't watching when they cut him
Out. C-section, you know. Green drape
Obscuring the mound of ripened belly
They extracted him from. He spilled
Out squalling, already starving. Still
Stitching her up, they fastened him
To her breast so he could feed. There
He rooted for the milk, so lustful
In his sucking that weeping roses
Grew from the edges of her nipples.
For weeks, they festered there,
Blooming bloody trails anew each
And every time he made a meal of her.
I know what you're thinking.
But he was her child.
She had to let him
Do that to her.

Molecules

Whether it's true or not, that all our
molecules replace themselves each seven
years, his body seems halfway new again,
one year into sobriety. I keep my distance now
but recall his painful, ten-pound freight, the torpor
of late-term pregnancy. All those final weeks, I rested,
famished, calling for food I could spin into blood
and bones so he could thrive. Even then, his cravings
ruled us both—mindlessly, he craved to grow,
taking what he needed from my willing body
as—two decades later—he would steal
what he needed from my dresser drawers—
bank book, string of pearls, his grandmother's
tiny chip of diamond-studded wedding ring.
The latter must have brought him almost nothing
at the Cash for Gold store where all the junkies hang out.

Driving

That was the year that summer lingered
and fall came on late. I was still wearing
sleeveless clothes when the temperatures fell,
and the wind rose suddenly, and tore the leaves
from their branches in a matter of days.

By then, there was a long line of addicts
on the corner every morning—red-nosed
and shivering, sores all over, reminding me
of the roaming packs of starving dogs that clog
the streets of third world countries. I shooed them
away when they begged for money . . . All that autumn,

I was searching for my son. Why I never looked
among the junkies on the corner who, after all,
were other people's sons, or why—*god help me*—
I drove right through their tattered clots,
and kept my coins to myself, and controlled
my thoughts—I have no clue. I just kept driving
though I had no sense of where I was going,
or what I'd do, or what I might find if I got there.

100%

Is what she'll never be
Again. Not ever whole
Or complete. Never fit
Tidily back together
The way she was when she
First was. Broken now.
Forever, it feels. All
Her inner parts re-
Arranged in new patterns
She can't recognize.
And though human eyes
Cannot discern the lines
Where the paste pot
Pasted back together
All the broken scraps,
She can feel the shredded
Edges cutting her inside every-
Where the paper tore,
Sliding under the surface,
Striving for realignment
With where they were before
The needle loaded up,
And pricked through skin,
And found the vein, and
Plunged. Before the junk.
Before the junkie who once
Had been her daughter.
Or her son. Before all
That. Back when she was
Of a piece. When she
Was whole. Intact. Complete.

When she could still believe
Her child and she
Had once been
One.

Support Group

For a long time, each day was a bad day.
Truthfully? For *years*, each day was a bad day.

The nights were worse, but she could slide
The deadbolt on the bedroom door, and swallow
An Ambien, or two, to summon sleep.

Thank god she never dreamed about it.

The meetings helped, but it was hard to go
Because the first thing you did was admit
You were *fucked*, and had no power.

Still: It was worse to stay home, sitting on the fear
Like a solitary hen hatching poisoned eggs.

There were a lot of rules and tissues in the room.
The rules were followed. The tissues were
Dispensed to those who wept.

Many wept.

In the rooms, there was infinite suffering.
It had 3 minutes each to describe itself.

A little timer went off, or someone waved
A cardboard clock face in the air. One Suffering
Stopped talking. Then the next Suffering started up.

A lot of suffering in the world, is the first clear thought
Most people have when they come here.

At the Meetings, They Say Detach with Love

When the alcoholic fell before reaching
The bed, and pissed his pants before
Passing out, and shat himself, and puked
Up what was left of lunch, and just lay there
Unconscious, soaking the carpet, his program
Practicing wife turned him on his side,
And left him there to sleep it off.

Whatever lesson she meant to share
When she told this story at a meeting
Eluded me. I could not make it fit
The rage-filled narrative I lived inside
That starred a drug-addicted son who
Jacked his mother's car and traded it for dope.
I settled for detachment minus hatred . . .

Regardless, love's cellmate—hate—germinated
And grew until the bilious pit in my stomach
When his name blinked into view on the iPhone
Screen had eaten me in two. For longer than you
Might imagine, I lived like that, the two halves
Of me detached, one from the other: heart
From mind. My body from his body.

Detox

So she wouldn't judge, she practiced empathy,
sitting for months in full lotus, palms open, thumb
and forefinger touching to make a small circle
she could empty her thoughts inside until emptiness
was all that filled her. To complete the ritual
she purified her body, deleting the nightly glass
of Spanish red she savored while preparing dinner.
Her medications—all prescribed—were next:
the benzodiazepene she seldom took. Trazodone
to help her sleep. The antidepressant she swallowed
every day. It surprised her—how long they took
to leave her body, and how reluctantly they exited.
They bothered her for weeks, waking her at night,
throbbing through the lengthy spans of muscles—
the quadriceps and gastrocnemius
complaining as her system forced them out.

It was harder than she'd thought—giving up
her little pleasures, taking the shine off things
she had gotten used to polishing up at the end
of the day to anesthetize their prick . . . Still
it wasn't all *that* difficult to shed those habits,
and she barely noticed any difference until
she saw him in the detox unit behind glass,
lined up on a bench with all the other addicts
and the drunks. They looked like convicts
sitting side by side, with their laceless sneakers
and their beltless pants, locked in and shackled
to beeping monitors and IV drips.

She was clean herself by then. So nothing
softened the blow or diluted the force of awful
feelings that slammed up inside her chest

when she saw that sight. She had to take it
raw because she couldn't rush home anymore
(as she would have done before) to calm herself
with a soothing dose of Zoloft and merlot.

Getting Clean

i

You can boil yourself down
to the rudiments, all the way
to the very bottom, and sit there
pruning yourself to the compact form
of a bouillon cube, its salty bite
stuffed tight inside, and *still*
be suffused with mindless craving . . .

ii

On the bad days, he said, *before*
I even get out of bed I have to pray.

I asked him if he would mind
telling me what he prayed for.

I just say, "Help. Help me.
Could you help me get out of bed . . ."

iii

In the middle of the meeting, an old-timer suddenly
yelled out, "Sit down and suffer, and shut the hell up."

iv

Hate to tell you:
the torment might
not dissipate. And
though you think
it might have sunk,

don't be fooled. It's
not a ship. Think:
tumor. Still alive,
still growing. After
treatment, if you're
lucky, slightly shrunk.

v

Shrunk or unshrunk,
the new thinking says
that craving lives on
hoarding its power.

Even the addicts
who are atheists
learn this lesson:
There is something
bigger than they are,
and unlike them,
it lives forever.

Relapse

Several of the young men
from the treatment center are
already dead. They spanned
the demographic spectrum
so no conclusions can be made
about why they did, or didn't, make it.
They just went back to using . . .

I remember their mothers
from the Family Program
where we gathered for a week
to educate ourselves about addiction
as "disease," and to learn
to not "enable," and
to practice letting go.

We held hands, and role played,
and chanted healing mantras,
and shared "experience, strength,
and hope." But in the restroom,
we dropped our masks and wailed
full blast, and held each other
and collapsed on the floor,
showing cell phone images
of our boys suited up for little league
and tumbling with their puppies.

Like every other addict's mother,
I have cried myself out, wrung
dry and ground down by the grief
and fear that fuel my weeping.
The single lesson I have learned
is this: A person can only feel

so much. Eventually, affect overflows
and loses shape as it escapes
from its container. If the thing
inside is hot? It scalds or scorches
every part of us it touches.
And if it's cold, it freezes.

The Power of Narrative

Even with the sprawling, unbound stomach
of midlife, and the lumpy breasts she doesn't bother
to hitch up anymore, something makes her shine.

So in my mind, I call her Gaslight Lamp:
the kind you find on the townhouses
of the rich that flame steadily, non-

stop, hooked up to some fossil fuel
source that energizes those generous pools
of light they shed, both day and night.

Like *that,* she walks around shining, lit
from inside but not by something shot
up, snorted, smoked. Years since that . . .

At a meeting once, I heard her tell her story
and had to step outside and take a moment
to clear those images from my head—

All that stuff about what she did to the kittens
and their mother cat . . . How would anyone *ever*
come back from that? But there

she was, and I could see her through
the window in her garish-colored
polyester slacks, her undyed

frizzy hair, and Walmart flats—
all her ordinary splendor—
the kind I never recognized until

I started coming to this room
with its cinderblock walls
and its stale smell of old coffee

where all I have to do is show up
and sit quietly and wait my turn
and listen to some stories.

Three Syllables Describing Addiction

Time breaks down, the therapist
Said in her practical voice, trying
To explain the nature of craving.

Time breaks down and stops
Going forward—it backs up,
Lurches and pools in long

Periods of stasis. Closed loops
Or broken circuits. *Yes:* addicts
Are fucked, and live out of

Sequence with everyone else.
While they're financing their next
Fix, robbing their own mothers,

Or screwing some stranger
Standing up in an alley, we're
Unraveling beside them, time-

Traveling ourselves all the way
Back to the start where it might
Be possible to blot all of us out

And put us out of our misery
Before this plot ever gets started
And pulls us into this future.

Metaphor-less

The dryness dead center
Of deep pain. The bone on
Bone grinding that goes on
For months preceding
The surgery—that's the way
The parent whose child is using
Heroin again feels in the middle
Of the night unable to sleep, standing
At the bedroom window, looking out
Just barely conscious of what the moon
Looks like—drained, gray. The moon
Is a popular literary image—solipsistic
Misery, misplaced love. *Whatever.*
Tonight, it's nothing but a source
Of milky light, swinging high up in the sky
Shining weakly on the bleakness inside
And the bleakness outside that has
No other meaning but the cold
Un-crackable rock of itself.

Parental

When the whole thing burst into flame
it burned outward from the center
and threatened the circumference.

The two of them were imprisoned inside.
They sat there helpless during the day,
and lay there crying every night.
Inside that ring, encircled by flame,
they prayed for fire's cleansing force.

They had read about it in the phoenix myth—
how the suicidal firebird strikes a match
inside its nest, and burns itself to death.

Then—in brand-new form—the bird's reborn,
reignited by an unextinguished spark
that survived the cooling embers.

That was the thing that kept them going—
the argument they had about the single spark:
whether to blow on it, or stamp it out.

Bikers

Heading east on Route 6,
A young couple scutters by
On a motorbike. *Harley,* I think.
On their way to the beach. I can
See his feet are bare, resting inches
From the muffler's burning heat—*oh*
The recklessness of young men
That makes them so exciting
To fuck, and sends them off
To war, whistling and marching.

I still remember both my brothers
As young men, and the motorcycles
They scrimped and saved to buy.
What foreign lives they lived
With their deer hunts, and their
Love of speed, and their boring jobs
In factories. When they jumped
The starters and roared off helmetless
And fast, I feared they'd lose their lives
weaving through the freeway traffic.

Wherever it was they needed to get
So fast, neither ever reached. One
Is dead now from drugs and drink.
And the other finally sold his bike
After it lay for years, disassembled
On the bedroom floor where his kids
Used to sleep before the divorce,
Before his wife moved out, and
Took them all away to another state.

The Brothers

The gap between them was five years wide.
So closeness had varied over time—some-
times homicidally hot, then cooling down,
but never fully burning off.

Growing up, we joked about the deadly way
they fought: who was Cain, and who was Abel.
Which is to say: who murdered whom . . .

I heard about the way they sat knee to knee
that weekend at the treatment center—
the other addicts and their kin circled round,
listening and watching. Someone told me
how hard my two boys wept, and how
the snot poured down their faces, and how
entranced the others were by what they said,
and how beautifully they said it.

I raised them in a house of books,
and taught them to love the written word.
Still, I declined to read the transcribed text
of what transpired at that session, even though
it's been my habit—until now—to follow
with my finger down the page, line by line,
and word by word, meting out the nuance.
Not this time. For god's sake, please don't
tell me what they said, or who they named,
or which one took responsibility for what.

Addiction is a family disease. It infects
each member and distorts their stories. It lives
to breech the boundaries of given texts,
and to change old narratives and destroy

plots you thought were set in stone.
In jealousy and anger, Cain slew Abel
in the charter myth. In real life, I suspect
that Abel also slew his brother.

Sibling Psychology

He's dead to us now—
our jackass younger
brother—the one we
ridiculed for being odd
and unlike us. But what
the hell. He was *our* weirdo
who yodeled arias while
showering, and loathed
soccer, and spent the whole
trip to Cabo playing Xbox
in the game room's dark.

Lucky you were born to *us,*
is what we used to say,
pushing him farther away
in that unhealthy mode
of dysfunctional attachment
that characterizes our clan.
Our problems go way back
to the old country and the bad
brain chemistries of all those
bloody-minded Highland Scots
who lived to drink and fight . . .

We passed along that lineage
of genes to him and bore
the consequences, and never
even threw him out—until
the end when he stole our stuff
and hocked it at Cash for Gold,

and threatened to incinerate
us all while we were sleeping
just because we wouldn't share
our Xanax and our Ambien.

The Daughter-in-Law

She called him the night before
to let him know she'd be there
early in the morning. Of course,
he called her an *interfering whore*,
and hung up on her, and got high.

She was there anyway by 8:15
and when he wouldn't open up,
the Swiss army knife she always
carries on her belt sliced right
through the window screen. I keep

Seeing her crawling in to wake
him up, and how she would have
entered feet first, and the colorful
tats on her calves and ankles
I'd always hated until then.

Turns out she also took a gun—
though no one ever told me
if she unholstered it to make
her point, or exactly what she said,
or what it took to extract him

From the filthy blankets on his bed,
or how she forced him in the car,
and child-locked him in, and drove
to the airport, and walked beside him
to the gate, and stayed until the plane

Had lifted off. She doesn't talk about
her feelings very much. So who knows
how much it cost her? What I know is

this: because of her, he made the flight
I'd booked. It landed in another state

Where his father picked him up
and drove him straight to treatment.

Plainstyle *Ars Poetica*

> . . . out of selection comes painful cattle.
> —GERTRUDE STEIN

For *this,* I need
a sharp-edged
tool to lend my
layman's hand
the confidence
a surgeon has
taking up the
scalpel. Un-
anesthetized,
I have to cut.

Thus, I slice
subjects from
their predicates
& dissect the
nouns to pare
them down
to empty
phonemes
devoid of
power. I
try to drain
the affect out.

*Poetry can be
a brutal art.*
Gertrude
Stein for ex-
ample: A

sniper in a
tree. All
amputation
& surgery.
Bullseye
steely
gaze &
butchery.
Steady
hand.
Sharp
knife.
Slice
the fat
that
rinds
each
word
cut
them
cut
them
down
one
by
one
by
one.

Dried Flowers: Vision at a Halfway House

When the full-flowering blossoms of early spring
Are at their prime, slice them from their stems
While they are still pliable and gorgeous. Before
They murder themselves with their own dark beauty.
Then bind them up in loose bunches, and carry them
Inside to the dry heat of a dark back room where
Televisions run all day, and cigarettes burn
Unheeded in ashtrays. Outside, the unchosen blooms
Will overtake the garden, and go on dying
Naturally, and in their time. But here inside,
The chosen few will be stored away, instructed to rest
For as long as it takes to achieve the dried-out state
That mimics life and keeps them breathing,
And allows them to hum their tuneless tune:

Not using. Not using. Not using.

Recovery

Nothing's the same anymore
now that the drinking has stopped
and the drugs have been flushed
from his system. Now that no one

who lives here is snorting or shooting up,
or coming home, deranged with craving,
or littering the bathroom with tiny bits
of balled-up tinfoil, blackened by flame.

Despite the brand-new quiet that forms
a fragile skin, tranquility eludes. Something
uneasy still moves beneath the surface
of daily life. Tentative, *nervous*, I strive

for rhythms that will make it right. In grade school
skipping rope, we girls rocked our bodies
in staccato time with the turning ropes, trying
to isolate the perfect moment we could jump

inside without rupturing the pattern.
It's like that now, I think. That's what
I tell myself, anyway, to keep my mind off
how powerless I am, and how I can't

control what he's doing, or where he is, or
who he's with, or if he's back to using. Every
time my mind jumps away from me like that,
I do the next right thing. I bring it back.

Ditto when I fail again. *Ditto* after that.
And after that. *Ad infinitum* . . .

Rethinking the Burning of Books

Regret is the only book I've ever
Burned: I threw it into the fire

As a useless text, and resolved
To stand still for awhile, and feel

The fire's heat, and not even try
To resist. The path backwards

Is overgrown anyway before we
Even reach its end. We already saw

Its sights and blistered our feet
And froze our asses off walking

There the first time. We know its
Start and stop. So why go back?

A bonfire built to burn regret
Destroys every pathway leading

Back, and wastes no energy lighting
Up the dark environs of the unknown

Future that lies beyond its flaming
Circle. Its message is fiery and

Stark: five syllables flaming
In the present tense: *It is what it is.*

A declaration, of sorts. A manifesto,
If you will. A way to live.

iii. Him

Willpower is nothing. Morals is nothing. Lord, this is illness.

—JOHN BERRYMAN

Reading a Biography of Thomas Jefferson
in the Months of My Son's Recovery

Because he bought the great swath of mucky swamp
And marshy wetland on the southern edge of the newborn nation,
Then let it alone, so it could fulminate, over time
Into its queer and patchwork, private self—

Because he forged a plowshare from paranoia
About the motivations of Napoleon, declining to incite
A war, and approved, instead, a purchase order—

Because he would have settled for New Orleans, but acquired
The whole thing anyway, through perseverance and hard
Bargaining, and not being too close with the government's money—

Because he bought it *all*.
            A half million acres.
                        Sight unseen—

Because he loved great silences, and alligators, and bustling ports,
And unfettered access to commerce, and international
Trade, and bowery, stone-paved courtyards, noisy
With clattering palms, and formal drawing rooms
Cooled with high ceilings and shuttered windows, furnished
In the lush, upholstered styles of Louis Quinze. Because he valued
Imported wines and dark, brewed coffees, and had a tongue
That understood those subtle differences, but still succumbed,
Thrilled as a child by the strange, uncataloged creatures that crawled
And swam and winged themselves through the unknown Territory—

Because of all this, I return thanks to Thomas Jefferson
For his flawed example of human greatness, for the mind-boggling
Diversity of Louisiana—birthplace of my second son,
13th of December 1990, the largest child delivered
            to the state that day . . .

*

Can't help drawing back at how he lived in two minds
Because he was *of two minds* like a person
With old-time manic depression: the slaveholder
And the Democrat, the tranquil hilltop of Monticello,
And the ringing cobblestones of Paris, France. The white
Wife, and the concubine: enslaved and black . . .

*

Before he was my son, he was contained
Within a clutch of dangling eggs that waited,
All atremble, for his father's transforming glob
Of universal glue.

From the beginning—*before*
The beginning—before he had arranged
Himself into a fetal entity, and begun
Growing inside me, he was endangered
By the mind-breaking molecules our ancestors
Hoarded, and passed forward in a blameless
Game of chance, shuffling the genes.

Even then, two minds circulated inside him,
Tantalizing a brand-new victim with generations
Of charged-up narratives of drugs and drink,
Of suicide and mania, of melancholic unmodulated
Moods, bedeviling distant aunts who died early,
And wild cousins who loved their night drives
On dark roads with doused headlights, speedometer
Straining to the arc of its limit, mothers who danced
On the dining room table, kicking aside the Thanksgiving
Turkey, carefully basted hours before.

We marveled at him in his bassinet—such
An unsoothable infant, so unreconciled to breathing
Oxygen, wearing a diaper, waiting for milk.
Still small and manageable at first. But whirling
Moods, baby-sized, and effervescent
As the liminal clouds of early spring, stalked him

Even then. Even then
    This Thing stalked him
Threatening his freedom
    And his right to self-rule.

*

We hold these truths to be self-evident, that all men
are created equal, that they are endowed by their
Creator with certain unalienable Rights, that among
these are Life, Liberty and the pursuit of Happiness.

—FROM THE DECLARATION OF INDEPENDENCE (1776)

Before we *were*
Ourselves he knew us. Explained us
To ourselves. Gave us a language whereby
We understood the restless grandiosities of our forebears,
And set us off on our well-trod path of personal
Liberty and greedy freedom-seeking. Minted the metaphors
We go on living by and misinterpreting, and clobbering
Over the heads of the rest of the world—Still,
His language stirs me up. Still, I believe
He was a great man, and seek in the painful
Contradictions of his personal life and public
Service, ongoing signs for how to live
In *this* strange era.

*

I know of no safe depository of the ultimate powers
of society but the people themselves. And if we
think them not enlightened enough to exercise
their control with a wholesome discretion,
the remedy is not to take it from them,
but to inform their discretion by education . . .

—FROM A LETTER TO W. C. JARVIS (1820)

Once more, we drive our son to the treatment center,
And sign him in, and watch him stripped of identity
And privacy. Shoelaces and cigarettes. Cell phone.
A dog-eared novel by Cormac McCarthy. A plastic bag
Stuffed with things we take away with us, and weep over,
Driving home. He has lost the safe depository of himself.
Is dispossessed. Is lacking any wholesome discretion
On his own behalf. Indicted by genetics, disempowered
By blood, how should we school him, except by love
And psychotropic medications?

*

Flight of ideas and verbal grandiosity:
Imaginary master of vast terrains, teeming
With fanciful creatures and fearsome weather:
A Louisiana Territory of a child's mind
Born there, after all, its doors and windows
Propped open to admit the gorgeous scenes
Of extreme weather, thriving in the rapid cycles
Of tropical heat, the coloratura of radical sunsets,
The tympanic symphonies of downpours
That dampened every day, and then were
Scorched dry by the blistering sun. Early
Symptoms we overlooked, and nurtured instead
As precocious tendencies of a burgeoning poet
Or a future president . . .

*

In the long nights when I can't sleep,
When anxiety courses through my body,
Racheting up to a stiff rod of fear and dread
I feel impaled upon, I sometimes let my mind
Drift to Thomas Jefferson and his famous
Inconsistencies . . . Here he is, tranquilly
Trotting through the bracing sunlight
Of national history, all long bones and red hair,
The eloquent incitements of his discourse scrolling
Out the documents that determined our fate.
But there he is at night, other mind in ascendance,
Tying shut the bed-curtains of a lover he inventoried
Among his personal property. With whom he made
Six children. Though legally he "owned" her.
And then "owned" them. His very own—
His sons and daughters . . .

The way that two things can coexist without
Canceling each other out—how did he live
Like that? *How does my own son live like that?*
As a schoolchild longs for certainty, I crave
An answer, and sometimes hold my two hands up
To weigh the *yes* against the *no,* slavery
In one hand, freedom in the other: a tiny exercise
In bipolarity that never helps.

*

Sometimes it helps to latch on
To someone else's vision
In a crisis—the way I did
At Monticello, so long ago,
Stumbling along the rain-slicked
Bricks of orderly paths. Working-class girl
In cheap shoes and plastic glasses,
Bad teeth. Terrified by the new world
Of the mind I'd entered. From the strict
Arrangements and smoothed-out edges
Of all those interwoven pavers someone baked
From clay, carted there, laid out by hand,
Brick by brick by brick, I carved a small sanity
Where I could rest. And read.

*

I cannot live without books, he wrote.
And so gave permission for a kind of life
Previously unimaginable: this life I live now—
Soothing myself and seeking comprehension
Among my many volumes.

iv. Us

As soon as you are really alone you are with God.

—THOMAS MERTON

The Punchbowl: An Elegy

Always be closing.
Vortex: a radiant node or cluster.

—LIAM RECTOR (1949–2007)
BLACKBOARD WRITINGS AT BENNINGTON COLLEGE

When I saw the punchbowl in the antique shop—
    Nothing fancy, midcentury, machine-cut, plain
Clear glass—a set of plastic s-hooks clipped to the side
    So you could hang the matching goblets from its lipped rim—
I wanted to break it without knowing why until my mind flashed
    Two decades back, to my old friend, Liam, and how,
In a flare-up once, in snowy Bennington, he called me, striking out,
    "A turd in a punchbowl." Afterward, he leaned into me,
Just like a boxer—but I never thought of stepping back . . .

That was the sort of friendship we had—one of us stepping in,
    Aggressive, to provoke. The other, refusing to retreat.
Jealous and bellicose, pugilistic, something sibling-like,
    In the way we reared up and clashed. Lessons learned
In the homes we'd left, walking out on poverty and trash when poetry
    Caught our ear, and turned us on, and helped us flee.

Liam was angry about something when he called me that.
    And nearly drunk. Well, who wasn't back then? That
Was how we shouldered through winter nights of child-size icicles
    Clenched to the steep slate roofs of the college dorms . . .
So it must have been one of those lung-hurting Vermont evenings
    When breathing, itself, was an existential act—

It was awful running home across the campus in the dark,
    With all those jagged borders of crusted frozen snow.
They frilled the edges of the plowed walkways, threatening
    As thick shards of broken glass. One inattentive step

Would body-slam you on the sidewalk's icy slick. We all did it—
        Fell down, rushing home, drunk or stoned. Frightened
Of the cold. Laid out, corpselike, flat, on a steel-slicked sheet of icy snow.
        Sometimes, in our poems or prose, we'd share the visions
That arose from that position, looking up, stunned and frozen, too
        Horrified to look away from the cold infinity of the punchbowl, upside
Down, filled with winter sky, hovering above us like a giant's centrifuge,
        Its inverted motor whirling, upwards, all the contents
Of the universe. Better to freeze. Better to bleed, and go on lying there
        And freeze to death than ponder what we thought we saw.

Well. Liam took things into his own hands, and died
        Early, while I went on living—still go on living, in fact,
With my dreary spans of rutted thoughts and stalled images
        (*Like turds in punchbowls,* Liam might roar) that snag me
In despair, and drag my loved ones along in my sorrowing wake.
        They know I won't do what Liam did—still, my sadness
Gives them pause, and mucks up life for them, and me.

My old friend's finished with all that now—no more dishes to wash,
        Or meals to make. No spills to wipe. No more carting around
The aging body's decrepit bulk. (*Pre-corpse,* he called it once.) No more
        Struggling with assholes who never had a clue. He doesn't
Give a shit anymore (if he ever did). He doesn't give a turd . . . Deal him
        Out. He's done. Dispersed. Shotgunned in a starry spray
Across the sky if that's a metaphor that satisfies . . . It does, in fact,
        Please me to place him in a register higher than he ever thought
He'd reach where his parts are jazzed with buzzing energies—
        A brilliant vortex emptied of the longing we call life, permanently
Removed from the misery some of us he left behind still struggle with.

The Diving Platform

Halfway across the lake's dark span
The diving platform glittered, somehow
Suspended on the surface of the water.
Somehow tethered in the depths.

It looked like an ice cube, he thought,
In a giant's mug of poison broth.
It looked like a tablet of aspirin, as yet
Undissolved in a sick man's gut.

It looked like a sturdy crust of cooked onions
Caramelized on the cooling surface of a bowl
Of soup. And it looked like a scab,
A monstrous healing, overgrowing
A wound that should have been sutured
But was left, instead, to heal messily, all on its own.

    *

If he started now, he could reach it
Before he had to dress for the ceremony.
Before he had to free the rented finery
From its cloudy shroud of plastic sheets, and fit it
To his body, tightening the blood-hued
Cummerbund around his waist, and clicking
Studs and cufflinks securely into place
At neck and wrists. Before he had to scrub

The unworn soles of the black dress shoes
To remove the words his brother had chalked—
HELP on left and ME on right—
So when he knelt beside her to receive

The blessing, no one would know
How he really felt.

*

For generations, her family had farmed
There, in the fields watered by the pond
The diving platform anchored in. And not one
Of those persevering men could say exactly
How far down it was, how many murky feet
Of water before he'd touch the bottom.

So when he saw her there, all the way over
On the other side of the lake, dropping her towel
And striding straight into the water, and shallow-
Diving in, and striking out for the platform
In the middle, he understood how it would be.
That he would swim out, too, and meet her
There, and they would sit together on the platform
Anchored in the deep, cold water for awhile,
Just keeping company, drying in the sun.

End of the Marriage

I buried the paper dolls
In the empty lot behind our house.
First laying them flat on cotton pads
And then sliding them inside
The thick white leaves of an envelope.

I dropped them down in a shallow slit
I had dug in the ground, and sprinkled
Some dirt over them, and walked
Back home, thinking, *Childhood
Is over.* Because it was true:

Childhood was over. The girls
Were growing breasts, and the boys
Were watching, their faces sprouting
With pimples and dark, sharp hairs
Jutting up on their jaws and cheeks.

After church was when I'd lay them out
On the living room floor and move them
Around in the shapes of life. Nearby,
My father was always reading his paper.
My mother was roasting the Sunday meat.

And all that time, as she basted
And baked, my mother was sleeping
With another man, someone we would
Never even meet. Maybe that was why
My father sat so rigidly in the armchair

Where he could see her in the kitchen,
Bending down to thrust the thermometer's
Steel skewer deep inside the browning roast.

Only she could see the center was still cool
And bloody pink—the meat too raw to eat.

Breast Cancer

He was a man of startlingly few words.

ζ

(She'd known that when she married him.)

ζ

Too late to back out now. That was what
Her mother had said, and her girlfriends,
And the priest, when she told them how
Lonely she'd become, and how she cried
In the bathroom after sex, wondering what
Had happened, or what it meant with no
Exchange of words. What she didn't share
Was how she wrote the words herself
So she'd remember what she wanted him
To say, tracing the letters with her finger
In fog she breathed out on the mirror.

ζ

Somehow life passes. A dream. A cloud.

ζ

Four kids had been born, including one
Who didn't make it. Both his parents died
In an awful span of two months, and then
The office downsized when he was forty-five.
Stolidly, he shouldered through, slashing a path
With nouns and verbs. Adjectives and adverbs
Were not his strengths. He was plot and predicate,

The sharp blades of language that mowed things
Down and straightened the remnants, and put
The world back in order, on silent mode.

She'd done what she could to mitigate the wordless
Swamp that sealed the space between them. Back
When it was young and sleek, she'd used her body
Like a compass to surmise his feelings, and sometimes
Slid over uninvited to his side of the bed, nightgown
Ruched around her waist, without waiting for a sign.
Or sat beside him on the sofa after supper
When things were bad, and stroked away
The tension bottled up. Over the years,
She adjusted her own desires, and silenced
Herself, and stepped back from all her needs.

Or at least she reached the point
Where she couldn't hear them wailing
Any more, and didn't recognize
How craven was her wanting.

ζ

Somehow life passes. A dream. A cloud.
Or these days, like the images of Instagram
Flaring up, then disappearing to become
Irretrievable forever.

ζ

You wake up, or walk out of the cloud's fog
And find yourself seatbelted in a vehicle
Beside a man who last told you how he felt

Three decades past in the stilted words
Of the marriage pact he obediently repeated
To please his family and friends.

ζ

Long ago, she stopped wondering
Who he had become, or how he felt.
Steadiness was what he offered—
Not a soundtrack of the process.

ζ

It's true, she admitted to her therapist.
He never promised more.

ζ

Use your words, she used to tell the children,
Chucking them under the chin with two fingers
And lifting their heads so their eyes met hers,
Teaching them to talk by speaking to them
In the foreign language of love.

ζ

He drove the pickup to fetch her.
And if she hadn't been so woozy
In the long jet stream of OxyContin's
Afterlife, she might have wondered why . . .

All business, he stepped down
From the cab, and grabbed her suitcase

And strapped it in the back. Then the nurses
Helped her climb up beside him,
And belted her in, and readjusted
The wide swath of bandages enwrapping
Her chest, and placed a pillow *just so*
To relieve the pressure.

ζ

For weeks now, she's been shooing her mind
Away from certain memories—the children's
Noisy sucking at her breasts, the sharp needles
Racing through her chest when the milk surged in.
How it felt to bend over after a bath, heavy
Handfuls of warm breasts, spilling down to fill
The convex cups of a lacy bra. The modest curve
Of cleavage nature had endowed her with.

Far back, like a locket's thumbnail portrait
Of a loved one who's been lost, she's enshrined
The image of his face as it was so long ago
The first time she undressed before him.
How his mouth had opened and closed
Soundlessly, and how she'd thought, then,
She knew what the words were, moving
Inside him, that he couldn't bring himself to say.

ζ

In the hospital, the nursing staff
Kept urging her to look
Beneath the bandages

And change the dressings
By herself.

But she could not.

ζ

Before the surgery, he shook the hand
Of the oncologist, and looked down
At her, laid out on the gurney.
And though he didn't say a word,
She knew he'd be there when she woke.

This is what marriage is, I guess. That was
Her last clear thought before she clamped
Down on the old longing to hear him fit
His feelings into words. She drove it back
In hiding, then dropped into unconsciousness.

ζ

Almost silent, they've driven all the miles
From the cancer center. Back there, he shook
The surgeon's hand, and picked up her suitcase
And shouldered the carrier bag bulging with all
The opiates and sterile pads and plastic drains
She'd need while she was healing. He walked
Beside the wheelchair without a word, carrying
The load. *This is what marriage is, I guess,*
she thought again—the familiar words ringing
differently through her brand-new, breastless body.

ζ

The Silverado was a good vehicle for getting up
The side of the mountain slowly. In first gear,
It could grind forever up a steep slope, never rolling
Back, or spinning out. He took his time ascending,
Avoiding the ruts, and while they slowly traveled
Up, she rested her eyes in the new moon's
Milky light, admiring the verdant images
Flickering past almost like a silent movie.

When they'd bought the property on the side
Of the hill, she hadn't wanted that much
Privacy or distance. But over time, she made
Herself adjust, and now she's at peace
With the silence of the woods, and how it echoes
Mutely the wordless years between them.

ζ

At first she thinks it's trash—the scrawling line
Of white markers, marring the grassy margin
That separates the gravel road from where
The piney woods begin their hillside creep

And wonders how they got there or why
There are so many lined up like soldiers in the dark,
And how they remind her of the cardboard sheets
The cleaner folds inside his business shirts . . .

ζ

He must have planned it, and written them
By hand, inking out each one of the three words
In black marker on the smooth white face
Of cardboard rescued from recycling.

And then he would have staked each sign
To a wooden shim, and hiked up the hill,
And shoved them deep in the ground, ordering
Those three words into one repeating sentence

She would read over and over, winding slowly
Uphill, strapped beside him in the truck's dark cab
As he drove her home after the surgery
So there would be no need to speak, and he could
Go on as before without breaking his silence.

Flying Home

Dumping the long weekend
out of mind, burying it
inside the clouds visible
from seat 17C—

Sorrow of fifty years'
duration scores large
stains in the sky, and
discolors the day—

Not only for you
but for those waiting
to welcome you home
with kisses and chocolate—

Innocent and un-
inventoried in what
transpired, still they'll
suffer its flailing

Weight—the dark wing
you're dragging home,
broken and bloody,
from the family reunion.

Longing at Sixty

An aging goddess
thrives in the dim
corners of my vision.
Silently, she flits
about, withholding
powers I once claimed.
And though the rinds
of cataracts restrict
my field of sight, I can
sense her smelly
presence, and how she
flaunts her tight body
and juicy parts, and
perfumes our common
air with erotic odor.

Daily, I palm my pills
for HRT and swallow
like a child just to
keep my hair from
falling out while *she*
menstruates, still
regular as a clock, her
beaded bags and
sequined purses
bulging with bloody
eggs she lavishes
on anyone she wants,
guided only by
libido . . .

Rarely do I see her
now, fenced within

the silvery crescents
that remain unsinged
at the famished edges
of my yearning. I would
murder her if I could
and bury her gleaming
parts so far astray
they could never be
conjoined again
to taunt and mock
me as they do, packed
inside the leather skirt
and stiletto heels from
which unreels an urgent
voice asking *Who has
change?* for the metal
dispenser of emergency
condoms that glistens
in the sharp-edged
artificial light of the
nightclub's restroom.

Dog Spelled Backwards

To see if the dog still loved me
I made myself forgo the sweet talk
I usually lathered it with, and screwed
The top on tight of the jar of treats,
And made it sleep in the laundry room,
And left it alone in the house all day.

Nevertheless, it kept the faith, and still
Jumped up joyfully when I entered, and
Licked me when I woke, and snuggled up
Beside me when I settled down to watch tv.

Who deserves that kind of love? Not me.
Love that keeps on glowing in the dark,
And never asks for anything back, and
Forgives old debts, and keeps creating joy.
The juicy, fresh-born smell of new life
Squirming in the whelping box. Love
That overlooks the cuffing, cursing blow
I dealt it when—still fastened to its leash—
It lunged against my knees, and knocked me
Down in the street. Then stood there, and
Took the blow as the bus roared past, zooming
Through the vacant spot where I'd just stood.

Epiphany in the Atheist's Kitchen

One moment her hands
Are soaking in the dishpan's
Sudsy warmth. The next:
She's on the floor, dripping

And kneeling. Bare memory
Of some great blow that
Struck her everywhere
At once—so heavy, she failed

Beneath its weight. Now she's
Down and hollowed out where
She can smell the trashy odor
Of the garbage pail, and feel

The greasy sheen of olive oil
From last night's salad, slicking up
The floor tiles where she fell . . .

In the abattoir, the slaughterer's
Hammer hits one true blow, then
Moves on blandly to stun the next
Dumb creature being shuttled

Through the chute to death. Not
Exactly *that*, she thinks when she
Can think again: not *death*—
Though something has perished,

And some strange force is rapidly
Advancing to occupy the newly emptied
Space. Whatever it was she never
Believed in before, she *has to* now

Consider that it really might exist.
Because here it is, beside her, right
Here in this room—not saying anything,
Not trying to convince her—just

Going about its business, removing
All the agony.

The Beauty

Beauty is magnetic until the poles
Reverse, and all that energy backs up
And forces itself in the opposite direction,
Filling us up with shame and sickness.

Then the ascetic holy man dynamites
The sculptures he used to pray before.

And the spurned lover tosses acid
On the beauty queen, his former wife.

And the novice painter, maddened by her master's
Gift, slashes x's in his canvas with a palette knife.

And what about the outdoorsman who used to love
The Appalachian highlands? Who has signed
A deal to blow the insides from a mountain
Where he used to hike? A corporate act
That efficiently extracts its core of gas,
But executes the ancient, untouched beauty
Of the verdant holler his bosses stole it from.

I wonder how he sleeps at night, killer
Of beauty, murderer of life. He should
Watch that online video of the West Virginia
Man whose county has been fracked. How
Beautiful the drinking water is, tumbling
From his kitchen tap. You can't even see
The methane pouring down, concealed inside
The stream until he strikes a wooden match
And douses it inside the flow that morphs

Into a mushroom cloud of orange flame. It bursts
And sizzles in the air he steps back from,
His arm thrust out to shield his dazzled children
From the broken vision of burning water.

Detachment

The things you love are still
Beautiful in the new dark
They live in now.

They're in their own stories
Part of a larger plot you're
Too small to see the sense of.

You can go on being unchanged
Yourself, still wrecking your hands
And throwing out your back, trying

To force open the window
That's been stuck for ages,
Or you can give it up, and sit

Still in the center of the room
And just breathe, and feel the grinding
Without trying to change it.

Yes

This world is a whirl of yes and no,
Of death and life. The living tread
Lightly and heavily the grass above the graves
Of those who once felt just as they do now—
Making love, eating a meal, raising
Wine to their lips at liturgy or table.

The sun is on our shoulders
In the graveyard, and it is hard
Not to exult in that warmth.

acknowledgments

Grateful acknowledgment is made to the Solomon R. Guggenheim Foundation for a Fellowship in Poetry that supported the writing of many of these poems, as well as to Vanderbilt University for a Poindexter Grant for summer research that also provided support. I am grateful to Mark Jarman, dear friend and treasured colleague, for reading these poems in manuscript, and to Ernest Suarez for his literary input and enthusiastic reading.

Poems in this collection first appeared as follows:

"The Addict's Mother: Birth Story," "At the Meetings, They Say Detach with Love," "The Daughter-in-Law," "Driving," "Metaphor-less," and "Support Group" in *Five Points* (Fall 2017);

"The Addict's Mother: Birth Story," "At the Meetings, They Say Detach with Love," "Detox," "Driving," "Getting Clean," "In the Midst of the Heroin Epidemic," "Molecules," "Relapse," and "Support Group" in *Vox Populi*, https://voxpopulisphere.com/category/poetry/;

"The Beauty" in *About Place* (2017);

"Bikers" in *Oxford American* (Fall 2018);

"Breast Cancer," "End of the Marriage," and "Rethinking the Burning of Books" in *Blackbird* (Fall 2018);

"The Diving Platform" in *Post Road* 29 (2015);

"Dog Spelled Backwards" in *Presence* 2 (2018);

"Driving" published in multiple formats by the Wick Poetry Center, Kent State University, including *Traveling Stanzas* (March 2018);

"Flying Home" and "Longing at 60" in *Miramar* (2016);

"Her Barbaric Yawp," in *Connotation Press,* http://www.connotationpress.com/hoppenthaler-s-congeries/january-2016/2708-kate-daniels-poetry;

"Molecules" in *New Letters* (Fall 2017);

"The Punch Bowl: An Elegy" in *Birmingham Poetry Review* (Fall 2018);

"Reading a Biography of Thomas Jefferson in the Months of My Son's Recovery" in *PMS: poemmemoirstory* (University of Alabama at Birmingham, February 2016); and in *The Mind of Monticello: Fifty Contemporary Poets on Thomas Jefferson* (2016);

"Sibling Psychology" in *Tin House* (Fall 2018).

*

"Molecules" was nominated for a Pushcart Prize by *New Letters*.

"Reading a Biography of Thomas Jefferson in the Months of My Son's Recovery" was nominated for a Pushcart Prize by *PMS*.

CREDITS

notes

John Berryman's quote is from *Recovery* (New York: Farrar, Straus & Giroux, 1973), 50.

Denis Johnson's quote is from his short story "Happy Hour," in *Jesus' Son: Stories* (New York: Farrar, Straus & Giroux, 1992).

Thomas Merton's quote is from *Thoughts in Solitude* (New York: Farrar, Straus & Cudahy, 1958), 113.

Gertrude Stein's quote is from *Tender Buttons: Objects, Food, Rooms* (New York: C. Marie, 1914).

Walt Whitman's quote is from "Song of Myself," v. 52 in *Leaves of Grass.*